Festivals of the World

SWEDEN

Gareth Stevens Publishing
MILWAUKEE

Written by
MONICA RABE

Edited by
NURUL AIN BTE ABD KARIM

Designed by
LOO CHUAN MING

Picture research by
SUSAN JANE MANUEL

First published in North America in 1998 by
Gareth Stevens Publishing
1555 North RiverCenter Drive, Suite 201
Milwaukee, Wisconsin 53212 USA

For a free color catalog describing Gareth
Stevens' list of high-quality books and multimedia
programs, call
1-800-542-2595 (USA)
or 1-800-461-9120 (Canada).
Gareth Stevens Publishing's Fax: (414) 225-0377.
See our catalog, too, on the World Wide Web:
http://gsinc.com

© TIMES EDITIONS PTE LTD 1998
Originated and designed by
Times Books International
an imprint of Times Editions Pte Ltd
Times Centre, 1 New Industrial Road
Singapore 536196
Printed in Singapore

Library of Congress Cataloging-in-Publication Data:
Rabe, Monica.
Sweden / by Monica Rabe.
p. cm.—(Festivals of the world)
Includes bibliographical references and index.
Summary: Describes how the culture of Sweden is
reflected in its many festivals, including the Feast
of Valborg, Midsummer's Day, Lucia Day, and the
20th Day of Knut.
ISBN 0-8368-2008-8 (lib. bdg.)
1. Festivals—Sweden—Juvenile literature.
2. Sweden—Social life and customs—Juvenile
literature. [1. Festivals—Sweden. 2. Holidays—
Sweden. 3. Sweden—Social life and customs.]
I. Title. II. Series.
CURR
GT4861.A2R33 1998
394.269485—dc21   97-31413

1 2 3 4 5 6 7 8 9 02 01 00 99 98

CONTENTS

It's Festival Time . . .

The Swedish word for "festival" is *fest* [FEST]. Swedes take their fests very seriously. It would be unheard of for a holiday in Sweden to pass without any festivities whatsoever. So, come and party Swede style—dance around a maypole, gorge on crayfish and sour herring, and make a bonfire for the Feast of Valborg. It's festival time in Sweden . . .

WHERE'S SWEDEN?

S weden is in northern Europe. Sweden's neighbors are Norway, Denmark, and Finland. These are called the Nordic or Scandinavian countries. The people of Scandinavia share similar culture, history, and language.

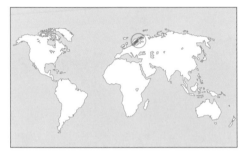

Who are the Swedes?

The original settlers of Sweden came about 14,000 years ago. They were hunters and fishermen. Sweden's first king, named Bjorn (bear), was a Viking king. The Vikings lived in Scandinavia for more than 1,000 years. They left their homes to take long voyages across Europe and North America on their ships. Modern Swedes are descended from the Vikings.

Swedes are known for their fair hair and pale skin.

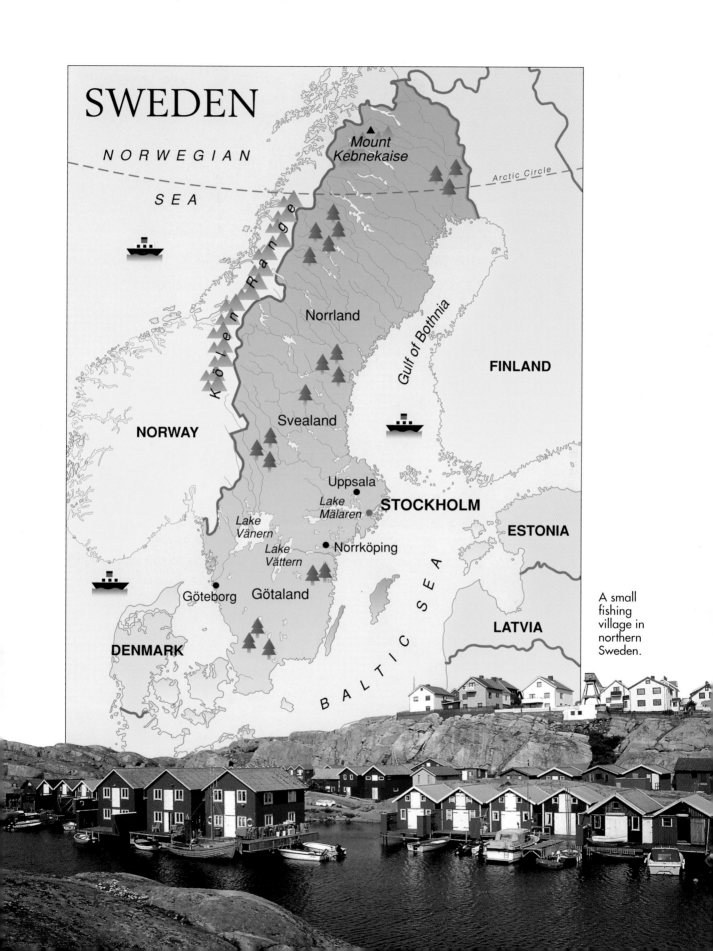

SWEDEN

NORWEGIAN

SEA

Arctic Circle

▲ Mount
Kebnekaise

Kölen Range

Norrland

Gulf of Bothnia

FINLAND

Svealand

Uppsala

Lake
Mälaren

STOCKHOLM

NORWAY

Lake
Vänern

Lake
Vättern

Norrköping

ESTONIA

Göteborg

Götaland

BALTIC SEA

LATVIA

DENMARK

A small
fishing
village in
northern
Sweden.

WHEN'S THE FEST?

Most traditional Swedish festivals are closely connected to religion and the changing of the seasons. Swedes are very close to nature, and they follow the seasonal changes carefully. In autumn and winter, the days are short and dark. But in summer, the sun doesn't set until late at night.

Can you keep a secret? Midsummer's Day is in full swing on pages 16–19.

SPRING

- ✪ **EASTER**
- ✪ **APRIL 1ST**—Children and adults play practical jokes on each other. The newspapers print comical fake news. If you manage to trick someone, you say the following verse: "April, April you silly fish, I can fool you as I wish."
- ✪ **FEAST OF VALBORG**
- ✪ **ASCENSION THURSDAY** Celebrates Christ's return to heaven six weeks after Easter. Religion does not dominate the day, however. Many Swedes make trips to the countryside and enjoy the first days of spring— weather permitting!

SUMMER

- ✪ **NATIONAL DAY**—Long called Flag Day, June 6th became National Day in 1983. National Day commemorates the day in 1523 when King Gustav Vasa founded Sweden. The Swedish king and the royal family join in a special ceremony in Stockholm, where the king presents flags to different organizations.
- ✪ **MIDSUMMER'S DAY**
- ✪ **CRAYFISH PARTIES**

What do you think of my beautiful "fish" hat?

AUTUMN

- ⭐ **ALL SAINTS' DAY**—This is a serious holiday when Swedes honor the memory of departed relatives and friends. Graves are decorated with flowers, candles, lanterns, and wreaths made from fir branches decorated with pine cones.
- ⭐ **SAINT MARTIN'S DAY**—Children carry brightly colored lanterns from house to house in honor of Saint Martin, the patron saint of the poor.

WINTER

- ⭐ **ADVENT**—Homes are decorated with electric **candelabras** and a luminous star of straw is hung in the window. Swedes light one candle on each of the four Sundays before Christmas. Advent calendars with 24 doors (one for each day until Christmas) are hung in schools and homes.
- ⭐ **LUCIA DAY**
- ⭐ **CHRISTMAS**
- ⭐ **NEW YEAR'S EVE**—This evening is celebrated with family and friends. Fireworks are set off when the clock strikes midnight.
- ⭐ **THE 20TH DAY OF KNUT**—This is the day when the Christmas season is over. It falls on the **name day** of Knut. Children have parties, dance around the Christmas tree, and finally take all its candies. The tree is then tossed out of the house.

How would you like to learn to play a traditional Swedish fiddle like this one?

EASTER

Spring usually arrives at the same time as Easter in Sweden. The days grow longer, and the snow melts. The trees begin to bud, and delicate spring flowers show through the dark soil.

Easter is one of the most important religious holidays of the year. It celebrates the **Resurrection** of Jesus Christ three days after his **Crucifixion**.

In their baskets, "witches" carry sweets collected from neighbors. *Semlor* [SEM-lor], cardamom-flavored buns filled with almond paste and whipped cream, are a popular Easter treat.

Witchcraft

Superstition and witchcraft are a big part of Easter. Hundreds of years ago, people believed that witches flew on their broomsticks to a place called Blakulla to meet with Satan. Witches gathered the day before Good Friday and returned on Easter Eve. To protect themselves from the witches' evil spells, people lit bonfires, shot firearms into the sky, and drew crosses on their front doors.

Today, Swedes still light bonfires from old, dried Christmas trees at Eastertime. As soon as the sun goes down on Easter Eve, fireworks begin flaring in the sky. Little girls dress up as witches, or "Easter hags," and visit their neighbors asking for candy. Does this sound like a familiar tradition?

Dressed as an Easter hag with a broomstick for transportation. Like many of her friends, this Swedish girl spends the week before Easter making Easter cards to leave for her friends and neighbors in exchange for treats.

Decorations

To celebrate Palm Sunday, birch branches without leaves are cut and decorated with bright, colorful feathers. In some parts of the country these are called "palms," because palms do not grow in Sweden's cold climate.

Other Easter decorations include witches made from straw that are hung over the doorway, and yellow daffodils cut fresh from the field and brought into the house. Just as in other countries, chickens, rabbits, and eggs are also symbols of Easter in Sweden.

Budding birch and willow branches decorated with enormous feathers are sold throughout Sweden before Easter.

Opposite: Picking daffodils to decorate the house at Eastertime.

Below: Easter eggs are an important part of Easter. They are hard-boiled and decorated with bright colors. Some families arrange Easter egg hunts for the children on Easter.

Smorgasbord

Easter Eve is a very special time when families get together and feast on traditional **smorgasbord** [SMEUR-gas-bord]. Smorgasbord means "open sandwich table." People help themselves to anything they want from a large buffet table filled with a variety of delicious foods.

Think about this

Three hundred years ago, many people believed in witches. They thought women who were different or had special talents were the devil's helpers and dragged people into hell. Sometimes, children were scared into making up stories about their mothers or grandmothers. The "witches" were punished and burned in bonfires.

FEAST OF VALBORG

O n April 30th, Swedes celebrate Walpurgis Night, or Valborgsmassoafton, the feast day of Saint Walburga. It is a very special day in Sweden for many reasons. Keep reading to find out why.

Greeting the spring

Walpurgis Night has become a day for Swedish students. It is celebrated in all university communities across the country. In the afternoon, students assemble for a traditional greeting of the spring. They make speeches and sing songs hailing spring. Then at 3 o'clock, they put on white caps to mark the changing of the season.

Left: A Swedish student wearing the traditional white cap.

Opposite and above: Choral singers gather around the bonfire to celebrate the Feast of Valborg.

Students' day

In some towns, university students make carnival-like floats representing events that have taken place during the year, most with political undertones. It is also a time for merrymaking and fun. In the evening, there are dances and formal spring balls.

Sing to the light

In many towns, people gather around bonfires at night to listen to choral singers welcoming back the light after a long, dark winter. It is said that witches gather on Walpurgis Night, so the bonfires are meant to scare them away. Bonfires also keep people warm since spring is still another few weeks away in the north.

King Karl XVI Gustaf in full military dress on his birthday, April 30th.

From left to right: Prince Karl Philip, Queen Silvia, Crown Princess Victoria, King Karl XVI Gustaf, and Princess Madeleine.

The King's Birthday

April 30th is also a very special day in Sweden because it is the king's birthday. Swedes come from miles around to Drottningholm Castle in Stockholm, where the royal family live, to pay their respects to their king. Children pick wild flowers and line up for a chance to present him with their gifts and to shake his hand. The king dresses in a formal uniform on this day, and military parades are held in his honor.

Opposite: Swedish children lining up to wish the king a happy birthday.

The Royal Family

The king is the head of Sweden, but he holds no political power. King Karl XVI Gustaf inherited the throne from his grandfather when he was only 27 years old; his father died when he was a child. Crown Princess Victoria, the eldest of the king's three children, will one day be queen of Sweden.

The royal family is very popular in Sweden. They do many things to help promote Sweden around the world.

Think about this

Lighting bonfires is an old custom. An open fire makes us feel safe, warm, and secure. Bonfires were often made to scare away dangerous animals, as well as witches and other supernatural creatures. People were afraid of the dark, and their imagination made them see things that did not exist. Have you ever imagined seeing things in the dark?

MIDSUMMER'S DAY

Midsummer's Day is almost as important as Christmas in Sweden. It is celebrated on the weekend nearest June 24th. June is when the summer nights are long, and nature is at its most beautiful. Trees are in bloom, and fields and meadows are filled with delicate flowers.

Above: A maypole being erected by men in traditional Swedish costume.

Left: Two Swedish girls dressed up for Midsummer's Day. They are wearing wreaths made of summer flowers on their heads.

Maypoles and flowers

Swedes decorate their homes, churches, and even their cars with garlands of flowers and leafy branches on the morning of this day. A maypole—a cross decorated with birch leaves and wild flowers —is raised in the afternoon in a field in most villages and towns, and in the gardens of many homes.

Dance and music

Families and friends gather to dance in a ring around the maypole and sing traditional Swedish songs. The singing is accompanied by harmonicas and fiddles. Many people dress in their regional costumes, and folk dancers perform special regional dances.

Dancing in a ring around the maypole.

Picking wild flowers to make wreaths and decorations for the Midsummer festival.

Midsummer food

Traditional food eaten on Midsummer's Day generally consists of pickled herring and boiled new potatoes served with sour cream and chives. Fresh strawberries with whipped cream are served for dessert.

Two men performing one of the many interesting regional dances.

Special Christmas markets open in December. They sell everything from decorations and lights to food and Christmas trees.

Think about this

Long ago, people believed every house had a **hustomte** [HEUS-tom-tuh]—a gnome that guarded the house. On Christmas night, a bowl of porridge was left outside for him to eat. Today, many Swedes still leave a bowl of porridge for the hustomte!

Santa Claus is also known as the Christmas gnome in Sweden.

Christmas food

On the afternoon of Christmas Eve, families enjoy a traditional *Julbord* [YULE-bord] for lunch. Julbord is a festive smorgasbord with dishes such as cooked ham, pickled herring, red cabbage, brown beans, meatballs, sausages, liver paté, bread, and cheese. The meal also includes a tradition called "dipping in the kettle," which means everyone at the table dips a piece of spicy bread in the broth left over after boiling the ham. Cookies and other sweet treats are served as dessert.

CRAYFISH PARTIES

The nights become longer toward the end of August, a signal that summer is coming to an end and crayfish season is beginning. In the shop windows, paper moons with large eyes and smiling mouths are displayed along with hats, bibs, plates, napkins, and glasses all decorated with crayfish designs. And of course, the markets display plenty of live crayfish! In Sweden, crayfish is boiled in salt water seasoned with dill. It is eaten cold with bread and strong cheese.

A man and his child brace the early morning chill to go out and catch crayfish. Crayfish are closely related to lobster.

Sticking to tradition

Crayfish parties began a long time ago, when a law was made to prevent over-fishing. The law allowed people to catch crayfish only a couple of months a year. The first day of the season was the second Wednesday in August. To Swedes, this became a sacred date. People waited expectantly for the day to arrive so they could fish all night long in their special fishing waters.

Today, Swedes can eat crayfish all year round because it is imported from Turkey, Spain, and the United States. But Swedes prefer to stick to tradition, eating their crayfish in August.

Swedes have made crayfish season into a festival of food. Families and friends gather in August for a feast to remember.

Surstromming, or sour herring parties, are held in northern Sweden at the same time as crayfish parties. There, people feast on sour herring, a dish that gives off a terrible smell to those who don't like it. But to many, it is a delicacy.

THINGS FOR YOU TO DO

The Vikings settled in Sweden about 1,000 years ago. They were fierce warriors who traveled through Europe raiding and plundering small villages. They were also explorers in Iceland and Greenland, and the first Europeans to voyage all the way to the shores of North America.

A carved statue of Thor, the Viking god of thunder and lightning.

Learn about Viking mythology

The Vikings believed in many gods. All the gods lived in a place called Asgard [AS-gard]. The evil giants lived in Utgard. In between Asgard and Utgard was Midgard, where the Vikings lived.

The gods made the first human beings out of two tree trunks found on the seashore. The man's name was Askr and the woman's name was Embla. They were the parents of the human race. The gods gave them three gifts—life, understanding, and the five senses.

A Viking warrior wearing a double-horned helmet.

The gods

The most powerful god in Asgard was Odin. He was the master of Valhalla (a place to which all brave warriors went if they died in battle), and the god of poetry, wisdom, and war. Viking warriors worshiped Odin as their principal god. Before a battle, they went into a trance from their worship. In their trance-like state, they could not feel pain, which made them very successful in battle. These warriors were called *berserkir* [BEAR-zer-car], which is where the English word *berserk* comes from. The weekday Wednesday (Onsdag) is named after Odin.

Thor was another powerful god. He was the god of thunder and lightning. Thunder came from his wagon when he crossed the sky. Lightning came from his hammer called Mjolner. The weekday Thursday (Torsdag) is named after Thor.

Balder, the son of Odin, was the god of goodness and wisdom. He tried to make peace in the world but he did not succeed. When he was killed by the evil Loki, the world perished. This event was called Ragnarok and this was the gods' last losing battle against evil.

Odin had two ravens that told him everything that happened in Midgard and Utgard.

Things to look for in your library

The Christmas Tomten. Viktor Rydberg (Coward, McCann & Geoghegan, 1981).
Favorite Fairy Tales Told in Sweden. Virginia Haviland (Beech Tree Books, 1994).
On Sweden. Stig Hadenius and Ann Lindgren (Swedish Institute, 1990).
Pippi Longstocking. Astrid Lindgren (Oxford University Press, 1945).
Sweden. (Transworld International/Journal Films, 1985).
Sweden: Nordic Treasure. (International Video Network, 1991).
The Vikings. Anne Pearson (Viking, 1994).
The Vikings. Pictures of the Past (series). Denise Allard (Gareth Stevens, 1997).

MAKE A JULANGEL

S ince Christmas is such an important holiday in Sweden, it is nice to make beautiful decorations for the Christmas tree. Angels can be made in different styles and shapes. This one is easy to make, and you can make more than one in a short time.

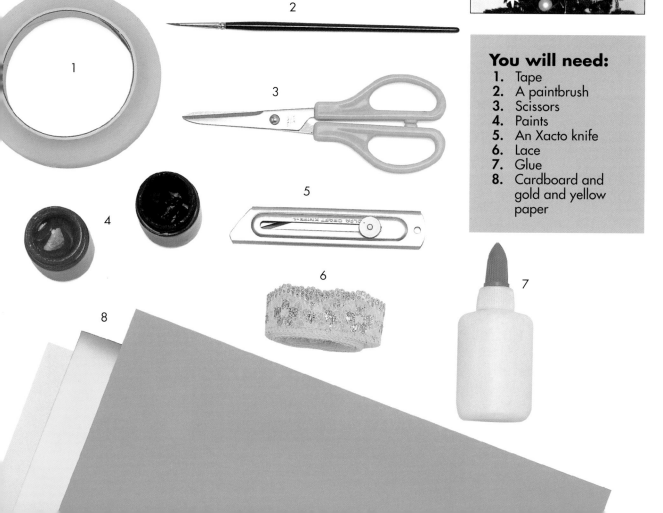

You will need:
1. Tape
2. A paintbrush
3. Scissors
4. Paints
5. An Xacto knife
6. Lace
7. Glue
8. Cardboard and gold and yellow paper

1 Draw a circle on the card-board 5 inches (12.5 cm) in diameter. Draw a smaller circle inside for the head and paint a face. Draw a line on either side of the circle for a tab and a slit.

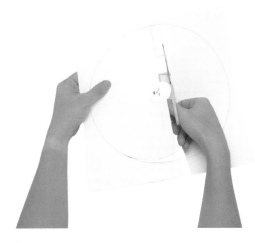

2 Cut out half the circle and the head. Discard the other half.

3 Glue gold and yellow paper around the head for hair and a halo. Glue lace around the semicircle.

4 Draw wings on the gold paper and cut them out.

5 Match the tab and slit and secure with glue. Now glue the wings to the angel's back.

MAKE COCONUT CHOCOLATE BALLS

These wonderful chocolate balls are a favorite with Swedish children. They are easy to make and they taste great! Make plenty, put them in a glass jar, and tie a ribbon around the jar. Give them away as a present, or share them with a friend!

You will need:
1. ½ cup (100 g) butter
2. 1 cup (240 g) sugar
3. 3 cups (360 g) oatmeal flakes
4. Coconut for rolling
5. 2 tablespoons chocolate powder
6. 1 tablespoon vanilla extract
7. 1 teaspoon instant coffee
8. A mixing bowl
9. A wooden spoon
10. Measuring cups
11. Measuring spoons

1 Cream butter and sugar in a large mixing bowl.

2 Add chocolate powder, coffee, vanilla extract, and oatmeal flakes and mix.

3 Make small balls the size of table tennis balls.

4 Roll balls in grated coconut. Put them in the refrigerator to cool before serving.

GLOSSARY

bedight, 21   To adorn or decorate.

candelabra, 7   A holder for two or more candles.

Crucifixion, 8   A way of killing people by nailing them to a cross. This is the way Christ died.

glogg, 21   A hot, spicy wine served on Lucia Day.

hustomte, 23   Gnomes that guard houses in Sweden.

Julbord, 23   A festive meal eaten on Christmas Eve.

name day, 7   Every day in the Swedish calendar is dedicated to a first name. December 20th is the name day of Knut.

Resurrection, 8   To make something come back after it has died or disappeared. Christ was resurrected three days after he was crucified.

semlor, 8   Special buns filled with almond paste and whipped cream that are an Easter treat.

smorgasbord, 11   A meal where people help themselves from a buffet table.

Sweden dress, 19   The national costume for Swedish women.

INDEX

DATE DUE